FABRIC FUN
for kids

Yolanda Gifford

A J.B. Fairfax Publication

EDITORIAL
MANAGING EDITOR
Judy Poulos
EDITORIAL ASSISTANT
Ella Martin
EDITORIAL COORDINATOR
Margaret Kelly

PHOTOGRAPHY
Andrew Elton
STYLING
Louise Owens

ILLUSTRATION
Lesley Griffith

**DESIGN AND
PRODUCTION**
DESIGN
Jenny Pace
MANAGER
Anna Maguire
LAYOUT
Lulu Dougherty

**PUBLISHED BY J.B. Fairfax
Press Pty Limited
80-82 McLachlan Ave
Rushcutters Bay
Australia 2011
A.C.N. 003 738 430**

**FORMATTED BY J.B. Fairfax
Press Pty Limited**

**PRINTED BY Toppan Printing
Co. Hong Kong**

JBFP 406

**FABRIC FUN FOR KIDS
ISBN 1 86343 243 4**

Introduction

My name is Yolanda and I am a quiltmaker. For the past ten years, my addiction to patchwork has grown. It has allowed me to stay at home with my three small children and keep my sanity. It is a full-time passion which my husband has fortunately come to accept and be involved in. We have three very creative and talented children who share a love of fabric. It is through their creativity that I began to explore children's sewing, beginning with basic patchwork classes for my children and their friends at home. I soon found a need for something more permanent, so I now hold classes on a weekly basis as well as holiday workshops where we sew, have fun and make wonderful creations.

The children's talent never ceases to amaze and delight me, and I am constantly surprised at the way we underestimate their abilities. I have come to realise that they can achieve their creative ideals and given the right encouragement, they do.

This book is written for the children, with their wonderful talent and freshness, who helped put it together. I hope they continue to teach me the art of having fun with fabric.

Contents

Know the basics

BASIC SUPPLIES

- scissors
- size 7 needles
- pins
- cardboard
- tracing paper
- pencil
- Vliesofix iron-on adhesive
- embroidery threads
- ordinary sewing cotton
- iron

EXTRAS

- pinking shears
- buttons
- braids and ribbons
- beads
- wadding
- craft glue

Running Stitch

Thread your needle and tie a knot in one end. Starting on the back of your material, push the needle up and through to the front, then push the needle to the back again, just a little in front of the last stitch. Continue in this way, going up and down along the material. Try to keep your stitches fairly evenly spaced.

Running Stitch

Back Stitch

To finish off with a back stitch, you will need to go back one stitch along your work. Bring the needle up through the material then take a stitch back, bringing the needle up again in front of this last stitch, then take the needle back over the same spot again. Do this three times. This stitch should be done on the back of your work.

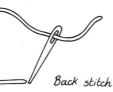

Back stitch

Overstitch

Thread your needle and tie a knot in one end. Starting on the back of your material push the needle through the fabric to be overstitched (approximately $1/2$-1 cm from the edge). Pull the thread through then take the needle to the edge of the fabric and push it through to the back. Bring the needle up next to the last stitch and repeat. Continue working around the fabric in this manner.

Overstitch

Tying Buttons

With two strands of embroidery thread, push the needle through the button from the front, then into fabric. Bring the needle up through the fabric again and through the other hole in the button. Take the two lengths of thread and tie them in a tight knot four times. Cut the thread 2 cm from the knots.

Tying a Button

Knot

To tie a knot, you will need to make a circle with your thread then push the needle through the circle and out under the thread. Pull the thread tight to form the knot. Sometimes two knots — one on top of the other — will be needed to make a strong start.

Knot

Batting is used to give a quilt thickness and warmth. For the projects in this book we have used a thin batting as the thicker ones are much harder for small hands to sew. Another thin batting, called pellon, can also be substituted for the projects. These are all available from sewing shops.

Vliesofix

This is an iron-on adhesive material that gives the fabric more strength and also allows you to sew without pins. It must be ironed sticky side to the fabric or it will stick to the ironing board. Always cut the vliesofix exactly the same size as the fabric. Vliesofix can be bought at sewing shops.

Embroidery Thread

I like to use a six-stranded embroidery thread in our sewing classes because it can be divided into two strands. This is much stronger than ordinary sewing cotton. Children can't always sew small stitches so it is very important that the thread be strong enough to hold their work together.

Fabric Textas and Markers

These are available from art shops and must be the washable kind. They come in different thicknesses and you must be very careful when you use them because they don't wash out!

Fabric Paint

Available from all art shops and some good toy shops. Many colours are available. Follow the manufacturer's instructions for making the colour permanent.

Fabric Dye

Fabric dyes are available from chemists. I use only the cold water dyes so no boiling is needed. The dye will come off your hands (with a good soap rub) but it won't come out of clothing.

Lazy daisy

Your little flower pillow will hang very smartly on a bedroom door handle. Boys might like to draw stars instead of a flower – just trace your shapes onto cardboard and follow the same instructions.

INSTRUCTIONS

See the pattern on page 8.

For the flower

1 Trace the flower pattern pieces from the pattern sheet. Cut them out and copy them onto the cardboard. Cut out the cardboard shapes. These will be your pattern pieces.

2 Place the pattern pieces onto the back of four different scraps of fabric and draw around them with the pencil. Cut these shapes out exactly, following your pencil line.

3 Place each fabric piece onto the rough side of the Vliesofix and cut a piece of Vliesofix exactly the same shape. Press the Vliesofix onto the fabric with a hot iron, pressing down for ten seconds.

4 Peel the backing off the Vliesofix. Place each piece onto the centre of one of the homespun squares in the following order: stem first in the middle, next the pot, then the flower and finally the middle of the flower. Iron, pressing down for ten seconds until all the pieces are stuck firmly.

5 Using two strands of blue embroidery thread, sew around the flower in a running stitch, beginning with a knot on the back and finishing on the back with a back stitch. Do the same for the flower pot, using two strands of red embroidery thread.

6 Sew the button in the centre of the flower using the tie method and red thread.

7 Pin the rickrack braid to the bottom of one piece of homespun, in a straight line, just under the flower pot. Using two strands of red thread, sew across the braid in a running stitch.

TO FINISH

1 Draw a line 1 cm in from the edge all the way around the unused homespun piece. This will be your sewing line. Place this piece on top of the flower piece with the right sides together and pin them together around the edge, leaving an opening at the top.

2 Fold the ribbon in half and place it inside the bag. Pull the ribbon ends up to the opening and pin the ends in the centre, with the ribbon tucked inside (Fig. 1).

3 Sew around three sides of the bag in a small running stitch, using the ordinary cotton. Turn the bag to the right side. Stuff the bag gently (don't overstuff it), then pin the opening edges together and stitch across this last side, going over both sides of the bag at the same time and turning under a small hem. When you are stitching over the ribbon, do a double back stitch to make sure it's well attached.

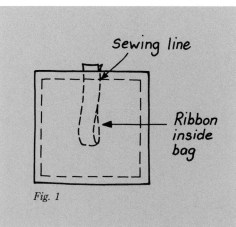

Sewing line

Ribbon inside bag

Fig. 1

YOU WILL NEED

- two 16 cm x 18 cm pieces of cream homespun
- stuffing
- 30 cm of ribbon
- 15 cm of rickrack braid
- scraps of four brightly coloured fabrics
- 10 cm square of Vliesofix iron-on adhesive
- button
- embroidery thread: blue, red
- ordinary sewing cotton
- size 7 needle
- pins
- cardboard
- tracing paper
- pencil
- scissors

Ellie's bird

This is the bird that Ellie drew at school. You can draw your own bird or you can share Ellie's bird.

INSTRUCTIONS

See the pattern on page 12.

Cutting

1   Iron the Vliesofix (sticky side down) onto the back of the fabric for the bird and a little on the red fabric for the beak.

2   Trace the bird and leaf patterns from page 12. Cut out the tracings, then copy them onto the cardboard. Cut the shapes out of the cardboard. These will be your pattern pieces.

3   Draw around the pattern pieces on the wrong side of the bird material. Cut them out, then iron them onto the centre of the beige felt in the following order: head, tail, body, wing, and lastly, the beak. Overlap each piece slightly so that no gaps show through. Hold the iron down for about ten seconds and press the pieces until they are stuck firmly onto the felt.

Sewing

1   With two strands of blue embroidery thread, overstitch around the bird's body and running stitch around the tail, finishing on the back with a small back stitch.

2   Draw on the legs with the pencil and stitch them with two strands of black embroidery thread. You can use a running stitch, stem stitch, or a back stitch as Ellie has done.

3   Cut the leaves out of different scraps of cotton fabric. For added interest use autumn tones. The leaves are not ironed on with Vliesofix, but are just sewn straight onto the felt. Ellie placed them at random around the bird, then sewed them on with a running stitch in two strands of blue thread. Remember to start with a knot at the back of your work and try to finish on the back also. Each leaf is sewn on individually.

4   Place the pieces of red and yellow felt at either side of the beige felt, so the edges butt up against one another. It's easier to sew this part flat on a table top. Starting at one end just do a big overstitch (not too close to the edges) and work your way slowly up the side (Fig. 1). Ellie used two strands of embroidery thread. Don't pull the thread tightly or the felt will curl, but pull it just enough so the felt lies flat on the table. When both short sides are sewn, sew the purple and the orange felt strips to the other two sides (Fig. 2). Sew the bead on for the eye.

To hang your bird on the wall, you can use Blu-Tack — one blob for each corner — but you had better ask Mum first!

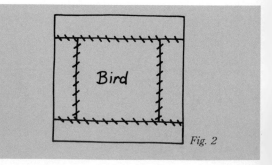

Fig. 1   *Fig. 2*

Bird

Cut 13

Leaf

1 – 2 – 3 chickens in a row

INSTRUCTIONS

See the pattern on page 14.

For the background

1 Pin the two smaller background fabrics together along one short side with the right sides facing. Using ordinary sewing cotton and a running stitch, sew them together with a 1 cm seam allowance. Begin and end with a strong back stitch. Press the seam to one side.

2 Pin the long side of the piece you have just joined to the other background fabric with the right sides together. Sew them together as before. Iron the seam flat and trim the background so that it measures 32 cm x 51 cm.

3 Cut three 12 cm squares of the Vliesofix. With the hot iron, press the Vliesofix (sticky side down) onto the back of the three squares of brown check fabric, holding the iron down for ten seconds. Press a small amount of Vliesofix onto some of the red and mustard fabrics as well.

4 Cut the ten small scraps of beige fabric into different-sized pieces, some about 3 cm x 5 cm and some 4 cm square. Place them at random on the beige background until you are happy with their position. Overlap some as in the picture. Take them, one at a time and, using the iron, press under a small hem all around each one, then pin them back into place. Sew them on, using two strands of cream embroidery thread, starting and finishing on the back of your work and being careful not to pull your thread tightly or the little patches will not lie flat. When they are all sewn down, press the whole piece with a hot iron.

For the chickens

1 Trace the chicken pattern from page 14. Cut out the tracing and copy it onto the cardboard. Cut the shape out. This will be your pattern. Draw around the patterns on the material with the Vliesofix. Cut out the shapes very carefully, exactly along the pencil line. Cut three chickens.

2 Peel the backing off the Vliesofix and position the chickens on the background. The pattern pieces go on in the following order: chicken body, the head piece slightly overlapping the body, the beak and red piece also overlapping. Press down with a hot iron for ten seconds when all pieces are in position.

3 Draw on the legs in pencil. Using two strands of green thread, stitch the legs on in back stitch. Sew on the bead eyes, beginning and ending your stitching on the back.

YOU WILL NEED

- 24 cm x 51 cm of beige fabric for the background
- 10 cm x 35 cm of a different beige fabric for the background
- 10 cm x 18 cm of a different beige fabric for the background
- 44 cm x 62 cm of natural hessian cloth
- ten small scraps of beige fabric
- three 12 cm squares of brown check fabric
- small amounts of red and of mustard fabrics
- embroidery thread: beige, green and black
- 25 cm of Vliesofix iron-on adhesive
- three beads for the eyes
- scissors
- pencil
- pins
- size 7 needle
- ordinary sewing cotton
- iron
- cardboard
- tracing paper

TO FINISH

1 Place the finished top piece in the centre of the hessian cloth and pin it around the edges. With two strands of black thread, sew right around the top piece 1 cm in from the edge in a neat running stitch. Draw a pencil line to guide you, if you find it difficult to keep your stitching straight.

2 Stitch around the chickens in two strands of beige thread, using a running stitch, to help the chickens lie firmly against the hessian.

3 To make the fringe, just pull six to eight threads out along each side of the hessian piece to create a frayed effect.

'1 – 2 – 3 away we go,
three little chickens all in a row.'

cut out 3

Angel light, angel bright

YOU WILL NEED

- small amounts of red, yellow, green, beige and purple cotton fabric
- 24 cm x 28 cm of white homespun
- two 6 cm x 24 cm pieces of blue gingham
- two 6 cm x 34 cm pieces of blue gingham
- two 4 cm x 36 cm pieces of blue gingham
- 28 cm x 32 cm of pellon
- embroidery thread: blue, light pink, caramel, green
- two blue beads
- two red buttons
- ordinary sewing cotton, white
- 25 cm of Vliesofix iron-on adhesive
- cardboard
- scissors
- pencil
- size 7 needle
- pins
- iron
- tracing paper
- pinking shears

INSTRUCTIONS

See the pattern on page 19.

Cutting

1 Trace the angel pattern pieces from page 19. Cut out the tracings and copy them onto the cardboard. Cut out the cardboard pieces. These will be your pattern pieces.

2 Place the pattern pieces onto various coloured pieces of fabric (see the picture for a guide). Cut the fabric in a square shape around each pattern piece, making sure you leave enough room to trace the whole piece later.

3 Cut out the Vliesofix exactly the same size as the squares. Place the sticky side of the Vliesofix on the wrong side of the fabric squares. Press with a hot iron for ten seconds.

4 Move the pieces from the ironing board to a table. Using your cardboard pattern pieces, draw exactly around each pattern piece on the Vliesofix side. Carefully cut out the parts of the angel.

ASSEMBLING

When you have cut out all your pieces, remove the backing paper and position the pieces with the sticky side down in the centre of the piece of white homespun. Place the red wings first, then the yellow dress, then tuck the green shoes under the edge of the dress. Finally, place the head just over the wings and the dress, and place the purple heart in the middle. Press the pieces with a hot iron, once again for a count of ten. Move the iron gently over the angel, making sure all the pieces are well stuck down. Now you are ready to sew.

SEWING

1 Using two strands of the blue embroidery thread, sew crosses along the hem of the dress. It may be easier for you to go all the way across making one half of each cross, then come all the way back making the other half.

2 Sew around the dress in a small running stitch, doing one stitch at a time as the Vliesofix will make your material stiffer and harder to push the needle through. Finish on the back with a small back stitch.

3 Using light pink thread, overstitch around each wing, finishing on the back as before. The other pieces are small and need not be sewn unless you want to sew them.

4 For the hair, use three strands of caramel thread. Starting at the base of the head, put the needle in from the top (you won't need a knot), pull the thread through until you have about 3 cm of thread left. Cut the thread you have pulled about 3 cm from the material as

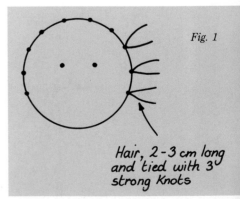

Fig. 1

Hair, 2–3 cm long and tied with 3 strong knots

well. Now tie the two 3 cm lengths in a tight knot, then do two more. Repeat this, 1 cm apart all the way around the angel's head (Fig. 1). (You could also use wool for the hair.)

5   Sew on the blue beads for the eyes, using the ordinary cotton. Make a knot on the back and bring the needle through the hole in the bead, going from the front to the back four times, then back stitch firmly on the back.

For the frame

1   Take the two shorter lengths of blue gingham and pin them to the top and bottom of the homespun with the right sides together and the raw edges even. Sew across in a small running stitch using ordinary cotton and with a 1 cm seam allowance. Fold the gingham back and press the seam.

2   Do the same with the two 36 cm lengths of gingham, attaching them to the sides.

TO FINISH

1   Place the pellon on the wrong side of the backing fabric, then position the angel on top of the pellon, making sure it's in the centre and sitting nice and flat.

2   Turn the edge of the gingham border over onto the backing. You can trim the edge of the border with pinking shears, so when you turn it over there's no hem to tuck under. If you don't have pinking shears, turn under a small hem on the back and sew lightly with a running stitch around the edge. Don't go all the way through — just enough to pick up the backing fabric. Tuck the corners under as though you were wrapping a parcel and continue until you have gone all the way around. Finish with a back stitch.

3   Fold the last two gingham strips in half and pin them to the front, 5 cm in from the side edges. With two strands of the green thread, sew on a red button, going from the top all the way through to the back, then take the needle back through the button and tie four tight knots. Cut the thread about 3 cm long. If you cut it too close the buttons will just fall off. Sew on the other button, removing the pins as you go. Now all you need is a piece of bamboo (I found mine in the garden) and ask Mum or Dad to cut it to be 28 cm long and you're ready to hang the angel above your bed.

God Bless . . .

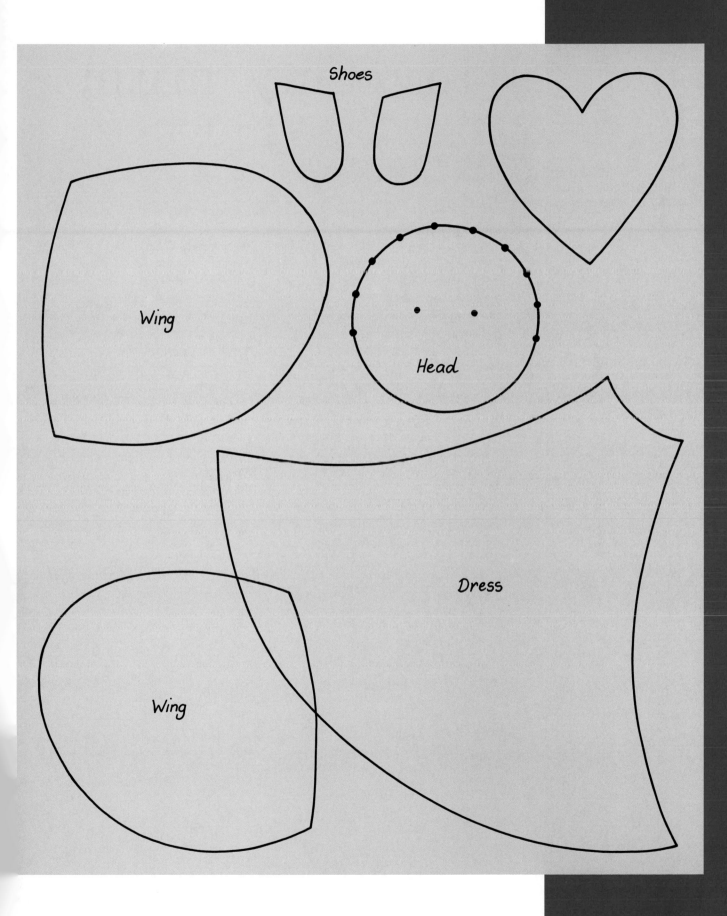

Shoes

Wing

Head

Dress

Wing

I love my mum

YOU WILL NEED

- **23 cm square of cream homespun**
- **permanent fabric paint, yellow**
- **small roller for applying the paint**
- **flat plate**
- **permanent fabric marker pens**
- **button or some beads**
- **23 cm square of thick cardboard for making the stencil**
- **sharp scissors**
- **cardboard scrap for placing under the work**
- **masking tape**
- **tracing paper**
- **pencil**
- **iron**
- **paling fence frame (see the instructions on page 79)**

INSTRUCTIONS

See the pattern on the Pull Out Pattern Sheet.

1   Trace the heart pattern. Cut out the tracing, then copy it onto the centre of the thick cardboard. With sharp scissors make a slit in the centre of the heart to the pencil line. Cut out the shape of the heart, carefully turning the heart as you go, so you have a cardboard square with a heart-shaped hole in the middle.

2   With masking tape, attach all four sides of the homespun square to a flat clean surface (like a table top) stretching the fabric slightly and making sure the tape is firm. While you are doing this, place a small cardboard scrap under the fabric so the paint doesn't go through and onto the table.

3   Pour a small amount of paint onto the flat plate and run the roller through it a few times to smooth the paint out and prepare your roller. It's a good idea to practise on an old scrap of fabric first until you feel confident. Place the cardboard heart onto the fabric and hold it down firmly with one hand. Mum or Dad might help you do this. Take the roller and run it back and forth a few times across the heart – don't push down too hard – just straight across from one side to the other. If you go over the same spot too often, the paint will smudge. When the heart is covered in a thin layer of paint, very gently lift the cardboard – straight up if you can – and away from your work. Leave the heart to dry for a few minutes, then press it with a hot iron, placing a piece of cloth between the iron and your work so the paint doesn't stick to the iron. This process helps to set the paint.

4   This is where you can tidy up the heart if the edges are smudgy. Using a dark marker pen, slowly go around the edge of your heart, making the outline as thick as is necessary to cover any messy paintwork. With other marker pens you can write a message to Mum or just sign your name and the date. Sew on an interesting button in the curve of the heart or do some fancy beadwork.

TO FINISH

You will need Dad to help you make a frame for your heart, following the instructions on page 79. When the frame is ready, position the heart square in the centre of the frame, then with a little strong masking tape at the top and bottom to hold the fabric, turn the frame over. Now tape all the way across the top at the back, then stretch the fabric slightly and tape right across the bottom. Do the same for the sides. When all four sides are firmly taped to the frame, cut a piece of thick cardboard, 20 cm x 25 cm, and tape this over the back of the fabric. This supports the fabric and holds it firm.

Now all you have to do is give it to Mum!

There's a flower on the couch

To fit a 35 cm square cushion insert.

INSTRUCTIONS

For the sunflowers

1. Sew large running stitches along the long edge of a length of yellow fabric in two strands of embroidery thread, starting with a big knot (Fig. 1). When you reach the end, pull the thread until the fabric is all gathered up, and stitch across to the beginning knot, pulling tightly (Fig. 2). Flatten the gathered shape so it sits in a circle. Make three flowers in this way.

2. For the centres, draw a circle with a diameter of 5 cm onto the cardboard. Cut out the circle and use it to draw three circles on the orange fabric. With the ordinary cotton and starting with a big knot, sew running stitches around the circle, close to the edge. When you get back to the start, pull the thread tightly. Finish with a strong back stitch. Flatten the shape out into a nice round circle shape with the right side showing. Make three the same, then put them aside for now.

For the cushion

1. Pin one of the shorter side panels to opposite sides of the centre square with the right sides together. Leaving a 1 cm seam allowance, sew them in running stitch using two strands of embroidery thread, and finish with a strong back stitch. Join on the other two side panels to the other two sides in the same way, sewing right across the two side panels already joined. Iron the completed square flat when you have finished.

2. Position the five flower stems on the centre square. Refer to the picture for a guide. Sew running stitches down each side of the stems, finishing on the back with a back stitch.

3. Now place the three yellow flowers on the top of the stems and back stitch through the centres to hold them down. Place the three orange centres in the middle of the flowers and stitch these down, going all the way through the three layers of fabric. Sew three yellow buttons in the centre of each flower, coming up from the back of the fabric

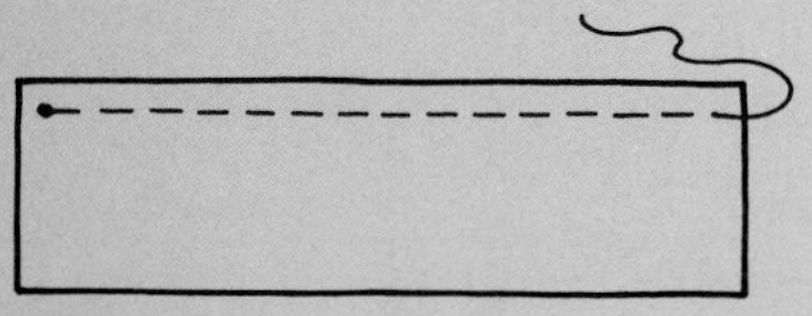

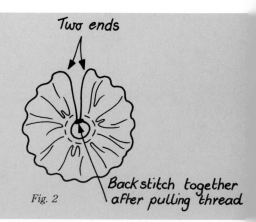

Fig. 1

Two ends

Back stitch together after pulling thread

Fig. 2

and going all the way through, up and down, four times. Finish on the back with a back stitch.

4   Sew five coloured buttons at random at the base of the stems. These and the four yellow corner buttons are tied.

5   Trim the edges of the joined square with pinking shears, tidying up and squaring off any fabric that looks out of line. Trim the edges of the square for the cushion back with pinking shears at the same time.

6   Place the completed cushion front on top of the cushion back, making sure it's centred. Measure in and draw a pencil line 3 cm all the way around the cushion front. Pin the cushion front to the back with the wrong sides together. Using two strands of yellow thread and a big knot (hidden on the inside) sew in small neat running stitches around three of the four sides. Finish with a double back stitch.

TO FINISH

Push the cushion insert gently into the cover through the opening until it's right down tight inside. Pin the fourth side together, keeping a firm hold on the cushion insert so it doesn't creep up. Try to keep the edges even as this is important for the finished look of your cushion. Beginning with a back stitch and a knot on the back, sew very slowly – one stitch at a time – working your way across the last side. You must keep the insert pushed down at all times or you will end up sewing it to the seam. It has a tendency to pop back at you! When you reach the end, finish with a very strong double back stitch on the back.

If you need to wash your cushion cover, simply unpick the last row of stitching and remove the insert. When the cover is dry, pop the insert back in and restitch the opening.

Ho! ho! ho!

Make this cheery Christmas tree pillow or picture and decorate it with special ornaments for your own special Christmas decoration. Ellie chose to write on her little pillow, and this is especially nice if you would like to give it to your teacher. She will remember you every year when she hangs the little Christmas pillow on her tree.

INSTRUCTIONS
See the pattern on page 26.

For the picture
1   Trace the Christmas tree shape, cut it out and copy it onto the cardboard. Cut out the cardboard shape to use as your pattern.
2   Iron the Vliesofix, sticky side down, onto the wrong side of the green Christmas fabric. Using the cardboard shape and the pencil, draw the Christmas tree onto the green fabric, then cut it out carefully along the pencil line.
3   Peel the backing off the Vliesofix and place the tree in the middle of the red Christmas fabric, sticky side down. Iron the tree, pressing for about 10 seconds so that it sticks well.
4   Using two strands of white embroidery thread and starting from the back, sew around the tree in running stitches just a little way in from the edge.
5   Now you can sew on all your ornaments, remembering to start and end the sewing on the back of your work. There are lots of lovely Christmas buttons and beads available from sewing shops which would be ideal to decorate a tree.

TO FINISH
1   Position the piece with the tree in the centre of the navy Christmas fabric with

the wrong sides together. Fold the edges of the navy fabric over onto the red fabric, tucking under a small hem as you go. You might find this easier if you pin, then iron as you work your way along, or ask Mum to help you. This makes a frame for your tree. When the edge looks nice and neat, sew around it in running stitches using two strands of green thread and hiding the beginning and ending knot. Iron the edges flat, carefully avoiding your tree decorations.
2   Fold the Christmas ribbon in half, tie a bow (make sure it's tight), and stitch this to the centre top by sewing up and down from the back, going through the ribbon a few times.
This little Christmas tree can easily be attached to the wall with Blu-Tack and makes a lovely gift for someone special.

For the pillow
1   Trace, then cut out the tree in the same way as for the picture.
2   Using the Vliesofix, attach the tree to the red fabric in the same way as for the picture.
3   Using two strands of white embroidery thread, overstitch all the way around the tree, starting and ending on the wrong side of your work.
4   Sew a star decoration at the top of the tree and decorate the rest as you wish. Christmas buttons, stars, balls, bells and beads all look lovely.

TO FINISH
1   Place the piece with the tree on the navy fabric with the wrong sides together. Draw a pencil line 1 cm in from the edge around the square. This will be your sewing line. Pin, then sew the red and the

YOU WILL NEED
For the picture
- 15 cm x 17 cm of red Christmas fabric
- 12 cm square of green Christmas fabric
- 18 cm x 20 cm of navy Christmas fabric for the back
- 30 cm of Christmas ribbon
- iron
- 12 cm square of Vliesofix iron-on adhesive

For the pillow
- 13 cm x 15 cm piece of red Christmas fabric
- 30 cm of navy ribbon
- 10 cm x 12 cm of green Christmas fabric
- 10 cm x 12 cm of Vliesofix iron-on adhesive
- pinking shears
- permanent fabric marker pens
- a little stuffing

For both
- Christmas ornaments: bells, stars, beads etc
- embroidery thread: white, green
- size 7 needle
- cardboard
- scissors
- tracing paper
- pencil

navy squares together, using small neat running stitches and two strands of green thread. Sew around three sides of the pillow, taking the pins out as you go. Turn the cover through to the right side.

2 Stuff the little pillow, but don't overstuff or it will not hang nicely. Sew up the open side, finishing off your work with a strong back stitch.

3 Fold the navy ribbon in half making a loop and stitch the two loose ends to the top of the pillow, on the back, with a back stitch. Make sure you sew it in the centre. You can tidy up the edges with pinking shears when you have finished.

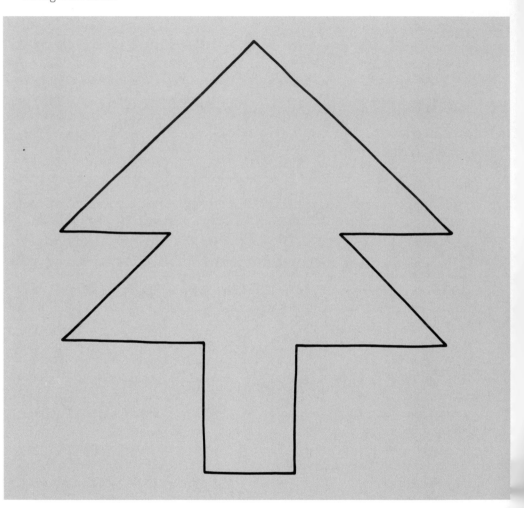

Patch + patch + patch

YOU WILL NEED

- scraps of brightly coloured fabrics
- stars and beads (optional)
- ordinary sewing cotton
- pins
- scissors
- tracing paper
- cardboard
- pencil
- size 7 needle
- iron
- masking tape
- paling fence picture frame (instructions on page 79)

INSTRUCTIONS

See the pattern on the Pull Out Pattern Sheet.

1 Trace the pattern from the pattern sheet. Cut out the tracings, then copy them onto the cardboard. Cut out the shapes. These will be your pattern pieces. You can, of course, design your own crazy patchwork by drawing a rectangle onto cardboard that is 16 cm × 20 cm, then drawing four crossed lines on the rectangle (making five pieces). Don't make your pieces too small or you will have trouble sewing them together.

2 Place all your pattern pieces upside down onto the back of your fabric scraps and draw around them. Add a 1 cm seam allowance around each piece as you cut them out. The pencil line will be your sewing line. Number them as shown on the pattern.

3 Pin the first two pieces together with the right sides together following the number order, so that you join 1 + 2 then 3 + 4 (Fig. 1). Sew these pairs together with a small running stitch along the pencil line,

beginning and ending with a back stitch. Press the seams to one side. Now sew 3/4 + 5 together in the same way and press. Lastly, join 1/2 + 3/4/5 (Fig. 2). Press the whole piece really well, pressing all the seam allowances to one side.

TO FINISH

1 Sew some stars and beads to one of the pieces, if you wish. You can add more or less of these depending on what you like. Each star must be sewn on with a bead.

2 To frame your picture, ask Dad or Mum to help you make the wooden frame. The instructions are on page 79.

3 Cut a piece of cardboard 2 cm larger than your finished piece of sewing. With masking tape, attach the top and bottom of the patchwork picture to the back of the frame, stretching the fabric out as you go. Attach the sides in the same way. Place the cardboard on top and tape this in place as well, first the top and bottom, then the sides, overlapping the tape slightly.

Turn the frame over and what a surprise! A work of art of your very own design!

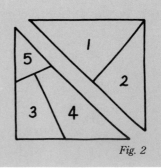

Fig. 1   Fig. 2

Dolly quilt

YOU WILL NEED

- twelve small pieces of different cotton fabrics
- 24 cm x 30 cm of cotton fabric for the backing
- 21 cm x 27 cm of wadding
- four tea bags
- large saucepan
- embroidery thread, cream
- ordinary sewing cotton
- scissors
- pins
- pencil
- tracing paper
- size 7 needle
- cardboard
- iron

INSTRUCTIONS

See the pattern on the Pull Out Pattern Sheet.

Cutting

1 Trace the square pattern and cut it out. Copy it onto the cardboard and cut it out again.
2 Place the cardboard square on the back of the twelve different fabrics. Draw around the squares, then cut them out, adding a 1 cm seam allowance around each square when you cut. The pencil line is where you will sew.

Sewing

The squares are sewn together two at a time and you will need to pin them together first. Then, with the ordinary sewing cotton and using a running stitch, sew the squares together in rows of three in the order shown in figure 1. Then sew the four rows together two at a time to make the two halves of the quilt. Finally, stitch the two halves together. Start and end all your sewing with a back stitch and make sure you always have the right sides together before you start. If you have sewn exactly along the pencil line then the squares will fit neatly, one on top of the other.

Tea-dyeing

Carefully fill the saucepan with boiling water and pop in the four tea bags. Stir the tea bags around a few times, then place the finished top and the backing fabric into the saucepan. Stir, then leave them there for ten minutes. Lift the fabrics out of the tea with a pair of tongs and wash them under a cold-water tap. Squeeze them and hang them out to dry. When they are nearly dry, iron them flat, pressing all the seams to one side, and your squares will have an instant 'aged' look.

ASSEMBLING

1 Place the top piece, with the right side facing you, in the middle of the wadding, then place them both on top of the backing fabric which is right side down. Turn the edges of the backing fabric over onto the top, making a border. Pin all three layers together.
2 When you reach the corner, fold one fabric under the other so that the corners are neatly tucked in. Sew around the border in a small running stitch with two strands of embroidery thread. You don't have to hem the edge, this adds to its 'aged' look. Finish your sewing on the back with a back stitch.

TO FINISH

This quilt is tied to hold the wadding firmly in place. Take two strands of embroidery thread and tie each corner by taking the thread from the front of your work (you won't need a knot) taking it all the way through to the back and coming up again in the same spot on the front. Pull the thread through until it's about 4 cm long and then tie four tight knots. Cut the other side of the thread the same length. Do this on every corner (Fig. 2).

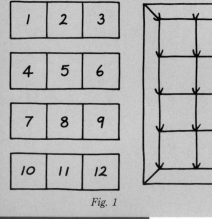

Fig. 1

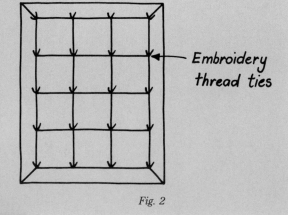

Embroidery thread ties

Fig. 2

Crazy about pins

YOU WILL NEED

- **small scraps of brightly coloured cotton fabric for the front**
- **larger piece of brightly coloured cotton fabric for the back**
- **embroidery thread: red, blue**
- **ordinary sewing cotton**
- **two buttons**
- **ribbon for the bow**
- **sharp scissors**
- **size 7 needle**
- **craft glue**
- **wadding**
- **cardboard**
- **pencil**
- **pins**
- **tracing paper**
- **permanent fabric marker pen (optional)**
- **pinking shears (optional)**

INSTRUCTIONS

See the pattern on the Pull Out Pattern Sheet.

Cutting

1. Trace the pattern pieces, then cut them out and copy them onto the cardboard. Number the cardboard pieces as shown on the pattern, then cut them out. These are your pattern pieces. Label the pattern pieces 'front' and 'back'.

2. Place the pattern pieces, upside down, on the right side of the fabrics. Lightly draw around them with the pencil. This line will be where you will sew. Cut out the fabric about 1 cm from the pencil line – do this with pinking shears, if you have them. Place the fabric pieces face down on the table and check you have cut out all the pieces you will need.

Sewing

1. Using the ordinary cotton, start putting the pieces together with a small running stitch and sewing exactly along the pencil line. A back stitch at the beginning and end of the row will make your sewing nice and strong. The pieces are joined in the order shown in figure 1.

2. Press with a hot iron when all the pieces for the front are sewn together. Now place the front piece on top of the back piece with the wrong sides together and pin them together.

3. With two strands of blue embroidery thread, sew around the heart in a small running stitch that is not too tight. Leave an opening where it is marked for

stuffing. You don't have to finish off the thread – just leave it stuck in the side, ready for further sewing, while you put in the wadding.

4. Stuff the heart with the wadding. I find using a little bit of wadding at a time much easier to handle than big clumps and the end result is smoother. As you are going to use the heart for a pin cushion, stuff it quite firmly. Sew up the opening, finishing off with a strong back stitch and taking the thread to the back before cutting it off.

FINISHING

Now you are ready to embellish your heart. Sew on two buttons on either side of piece 1 and glue on a little bow at the top with the craft glue. For the cross stitch, take two strands of the red thread and work your way across the heart in a slanting stitch, then turn around and work your way back, crossing each of the slanting stitches as you go, making crosses. You can add your name, but remember to use only fabric marker pens.

Pop in a pin or two and away you go!

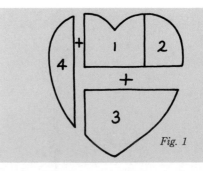

Fig. 1

Ben's glove puppet

YOU WILL NEED

- 25 cm of natural homespun
- 15 cm x 32 cm of red striped cotton
- 15 cm x 20 cm of pellon
- one ball each of medium green and dark green wool
- scraps of felt: yellow, red, blue
- craft glue
- small scrap of black homespun
- permanent fabric marker pens
- two large buttons
- pins
- scissors
- size 7 needle
- embroidery thread: white, orange
- ordinary sewing cotton
- iron
- cardboard
- pencil
- tracing paper

INSTRUCTIONS

See the pattern on the Pull Out Pattern Sheet.

1 Trace all the shapes and cut out the tracings. Copy them onto the cardboard and cut them out. These will be your pattern pieces.

2 Place the pattern for the top part of the clown onto the homespun. Draw around the shape, then cut it out twice, adding a 1 cm seam allowance when you cut. The pencil line will be your sewing line. If you fold the fabric over double, you can cut both pieces at once.

2 Fold the striped fabric over double with the right sides together. Place the pattern for the bottom part of the clown onto the fabric, making sure the stripes run down and not around the puppet. Cut two pieces with a 1 cm seam allowance.

3 Pin one top and one bottom piece together on the joining line with the right sides together. Stitch along the pencil line in a running stitch, using two strands of white embroidery thread. Press the seam down. Repeat for the other side of the puppet.

For the face

1 Before sewing the puppet together you must decorate the face. Make a pattern for the bow-tie, then cut it out of the black homespun, cutting exactly along the pattern line. Position the bow-tie at the centre of the top edge of the red striped fabric. Stitch around the bow-tie in a running stitch, using orange thread. Tie a large button in the centre and another one underneath.

2 Make patterns for all the facial features, then very carefully cut them out of felt along the pattern line. Place them on the top section above the bow-tie. Glue them in place with the craft glue, making sure you squeeze a little glue all the way around the shapes so that no edges come up. Press down hard on the shape and hold it for a few seconds. The eyebrows and laugh lines around the eyes are added with the fabric marker pens.

ASSEMBLING

1 When the face is completely dry, place the pieces with the right sides together and pin them along the pencil line where you will sew. Start your running stitch with a back stitch and a strong knot so your work doesn't pull undone. Using two strands of white embroidery floss for strength, start sewing at the bottom of the striped fabric on one side and end at the bottom of the striped fabric on the other side. Of course, a sewing machine would be ideal for this part so maybe if Mum isn't too busy, she might help out! Carefully turn the puppet the right way out.

For the lining

For the lining bag, cut around the pattern on the homespun and then the pellon, cutting exactly along the line. Cut two of each. Sew the two lining pieces together with a 1 cm seam. The lining must be a little smaller than the main glove to fit the pellon in between.

When you have finished sewing the lining, don't turn it the right way out, just slip it inside the glove with the two pellon pieces on either side, gently pushing your hand into the glove, easing the pellon with your other hand as you go. You might find it easier to put the two gloves together, then slip the pellon straight down the front and back, pushing everything flat as you go.

TO FINISH

When the three layers are nice and flat, measure up 2 cm from the bottom and sew them together right around the glove with a running stitch in two strands of black thread. Finish on the inside with a strong back stitch.

For the hair

1   You will need seven ties for around the head. Measure the positions from the pattern and mark them with a pencil on the top of the head. Cut seven homespun strips, each 1.5 cm x 10 cm. Fold each one in half and back stitch one to each pencil mark (Fig. 1). Place one hand inside the glove while you are sewing, to give you support.

2   Cut seven bundles of hair. Each bundle consists of twelve pieces of medium green and twelve pieces of dark green wool, each 15 cm long. Put the two colours together and place the bunch in the middle of a homespun strip. Tie the homespun into a tight knot around the wool. Continue around the head until all the bundles are tied. Of course, if you don't have green wool, then purple, orange, or any other colour will be just as nice, or maybe you could make different-coloured clowns – one for each hand!

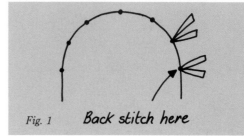

Fig. 1   Back stitch here

Tie + dye a cushion

INSTRUCTIONS
See the patterns on page 38.

For the dyeing

1 Following the instructions on the packet for mixing the dyes, fill one bucket with the yellow dye. Fold one 40 cm square of homespun and the 46 cm square of homespun in half, then in half again. Pull each piece into a long tube shape and wrap separate lengths of the string tightly around it, every 3-5 cm. The string must be very tight or the dye will soak through. Wet the fabric under a cold-water tap, then pop both pieces into the yellow dye bath. Push them well under the dye (with a wooden spoon) so the dye soaks through. When the dye is ready (according to the instructions on the pack), take out the fabric, cut off the string, then rinse it under cold water and hang it outside to dry.

2 When both pieces of fabric are dry, prepare your second colours – one bucket of orange dye and one bucket of red dye. Tie each yellow piece as you did before, then place the 40 cm square into the orange dye bath and the larger square into the red one. Using the same method as for the yellow dye, complete the dyeing process and hang the fabrics out to dry. When they are dry, iron them both.

For the stencil

1 Prepare the smaller dyed square for stencilling by taping it to a smooth, flat tabletop, stretching it as you go. Tape all four sides down, placing a piece of cardboard under the fabric so the table isn't marked.

2 Trace the two star patterns and cut out the tracings. Copy each one onto a thick 15 cm square of cardboard. Using sharp scissors, cut a hole in the centre of the star. Cut out to the pencil line, then carefully cut around the star shape so that you have a star-shaped hole in the middle of the cardboard.

3 Pour out some of the green and blue fabric paints, each onto a separate saucer. Run the roller through the paint a few times to smooth it out. It's a good idea to practise rolling the paint on a scrap of fabric first, before you begin your cushion. Hold the cardboard star template down firmly with one hand and roller across from one side to the other, trying not to go over the same spot too many times. When all the stars are finished, remove the tape and hang the piece outside to dry.

TO FINISH

1 Place the stencilled top (right side up) on top of the wadding, then place both on top of the plain homespun square. Pin all three layers together. With the star template, draw a few extra stars around the stencilled ones, but make sure your cardboard is dry before you use it.

2 Using two strands of red embroidery thread, sew in running stitch around the stars, going through all three layers of fabric and beginning and ending on the back. Don't pull the thread tight or the stars will pucker.

YOU WILL NEED
- two 40 cm squares of cream homespun
- one 46 cm square of cream homespun
- one 40 cm square of wadding
- cold-water dye: red, yellow, orange (available at chemists)
- 35 cm square cushion insert
- fabric paint: blue, green
- small paint roller (available at art supply shops)
- assorted permanent fabric marker pens
- embroidery thread: red, green
- size 7 needle
- scissors
- pins
- thick cardboard
- string
- two clean buckets for the dyeing
- iron
- masking tape
- tracing paper
- pencil
- wooden spoon
- two saucers

3   Measure in and draw a pencil line 3 cm all the way around the square. With the ordinary cotton, baste in a large running stitch around this line. You will take this stitch out when you have finished.

4   Place the top piece in the centre of the large dyed square with the wrong sides together and pin them together along the basting line. With two strands of the green embroidery thread and starting with a double back stitch, sew in a neat, small running stitch around three sides, making sure you go all the way through to the back for each stitch. Take one stitch at a time, sewing on top of the basting stitch. When three sides are completed, finish with a strong back stitch.

5   Stuff the cushion insert down gently into the cover, pushing it all the way into the corners. Hold the insert down and pin across the last side, then sew across in a small running stitch, holding the insert down with one hand while sewing with the other. This does feel a little awkward, but if you hold the cushion down on your lap, it will be easier to sew. Finish with a double back stitch on the back.

6   To add extra colour to your cushion cover, draw a zigzag pattern on the edge flap with the marker pens and don't forget to write your name and age on the back!

Note: It is best to hand-wash your cushion cover, if it needs to be cleaned. Remove the insert by undoing the last row of stitching.

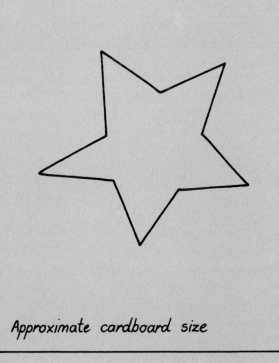

Approximate cardboard size

Star Stencils — large and small

Nick-nack sew a patch

- 28 cm x 64 cm of red gingham
- 25 cm x 70 cm of black homespun
- 26 cm x 60 cm of wadding
- two 5 cm x 23 cm strips of black gingham, (cut with pinking shears)
- 11 cm square of green gingham (cut with pinking shears)
- 11 cm square of blue gingham (cut with pinking shears)
- 4 cm x 11 cm of natural homespun for the name tag (cut with pinking shears)
- permanent fabric marker pen
- embroidery thread: black, white, green
- two buttons
- scissors
- pins
- two 1 m lengths of black cord
- scraps of cotton fabric for the hearts, two plains and three checks
- pinking shears
- safety pin
- pencil
- tracing paper (optional)

This bag can be used to carry all your sewing bits and pieces or your buttons and beads, or can be used as an overnight bag.

INSTRUCTIONS

See the patterns on page 42.

1   Fold the red gingham fabric in half and iron the fold. This is the bottom of your bag. Now open out the fabric into one long piece. Position the blue and green squares about 3 cm up from the bottom line on one side and pin.

2   Draw or trace three hearts, then cut them out of the scraps of check fabric, using the pinking shears. Pin them on the other side of the bag. Place them so, when you fold the bag again, the hearts are facing the right way up.

3   Sew around the squares in a running stitch, using two strands of the black embroidery thread. Sew around the hearts on the other side in the same way.

4   Using a running stitch and two strands of black embroidery thread, sew on the name tag about 2 cm above the squares, keeping it straight with the top of the bag.

5   Measure 4 cm down from the top of the bag, back and front. Pin one black gingham strip on each side, making sure they are in the middle. Sew the strips in place about 1 cm in from the long side edges, using two strands of black embroidery thread, starting and ending with a back stitch. Leave the ends open (Fig. 1).

6   Draw or trace two hearts for the squares. Cut them out of the scraps of plain material. Using white thread, sew these in place in running stitch. Finish sewing on the back of your work. Tie a button in the middle of each heart with green thread, leaving ends 2 cm long.

7   Cut three 18 cm lengths of the black embroidery thread. Using all six strands tie a bow for each check fabric heart on the back of the bag. Stitch them on by just sewing over the centre of the bow.

8   Write your name on the name tag, using the marker pen, or you can embroider it if you wish.

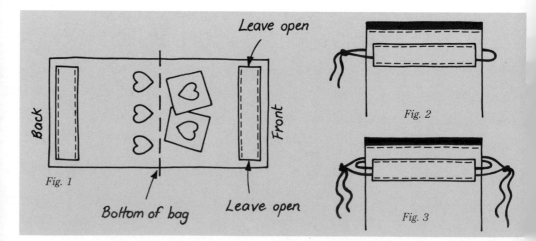

Leave open

Back

Front

Fig. 1

Bottom of bag

Leave open

Fig. 2

Fig. 3

ASSEMBLING

1 Fold the red gingham in half again, but this time putting the right sides together. Stitch the sides using two strands of thread and a small running stitch. Start with a strong back stitch, go all the way down one side about 1 cm in from the edge and finish with a back stitch. Repeat for the other side. Turn the bag right side out.

2 Fold 1 cm at the top down to the inside and press with a hot iron. Gently push the wadding down inside the bag against the sides. This takes a little time so be patient and gentle on your wadding.

3 Sew down the sides of the black homespun in exactly the same way as you did for the main bag. Place the black lining inside the red bag so the seams are not showing and the seams are matching on the sides. If you push your fingers around the bag you will feel the wadding and be able to smooth out any lumps or bumps. You should now have a red bag (right side out) with wadding next and then the inner black bag all in one round piece. Fold the black material down, covering any wadding that might be showing and tucking it under the ironed edge of the red gingham. Leave about 2 cm of the black material showing. Pin the edge of the red bag to the black bag. Using a running stitch and two strands of black thread, stitch around the bag, close to the top of the red fabric. Finish with a back stitch inside the bag.

TO FINISH

Place a safety pin at one end of one piece of black cord. Thread the cord all the way around the bag, starting and finishing at the same end. Knot these ends together (Fig. 2). Thread the other piece of cord through from the opposite end, go all the way around and tie the ends together (Fig. 3).

Front Heart

Back Heart

Home, sweet home

INSTRUCTIONS

See the pattern on the Pull Out Pattern Sheet.

1   Trace the main pattern pieces from the pattern sheet. Cut them out, then copy them onto the cardboard. Number each piece as shown.

2   Place the pattern pieces on the back of your fabric pieces, making sure all the pieces are placed with the numbers facing you. (Don't worry about the door, window and chimney yet.) Draw around the pattern pieces, then cut them out 1 cm from the pencil line. The pencil line is where you will sew.

3   Pin and sew two pieces together at a time with ordinary sewing cotton, stitching them together using a small running stitch and beginning and ending with a back stitch. Follow the order indicated in figures 1-6. When the house is sewn together, press all the seams to one side with a hot iron.

4   Iron a small piece of Vliesofix (sticky side down) onto the back of three different fabrics for the door, window and chimney, pressing down for ten seconds. Make patterns for these pieces, then draw around them on the Vliesofix side. Cut them out exactly along the pencil line. Peel away the backing from the Vliesofix and iron the pieces into position on the house, holding the iron down for ten seconds. With two strands of embroidery thread, overstitch around the door, window and chimney in different colours, beginning and ending on the back of your work.

5   Place the check backing fabric face down with the pellon on top. Place the top piece (right side up) in the middle of the pellon. The backing fabric will be larger than the top. Pin the layers together, then fold the edges of the backing onto the top, tucking in the corners as you go. If you cut the edge of the check fabric with pinking shears, you won't need to turn under a hem and this makes it easier to sew. Using two strands of black embroidery thread and small neat running stitches, sew all the way around, beginning and ending on the back. This stitch should go all the way through to the back and holds the three layers together. Work on a flat table top and make sure you don't pull the thread tightly or the house will not hang straight.

TO FINISH

Cut or tear two hanging strips in black fabric, each 4 cm x 20 cm. Fold them in half, then pin them along the fold line to the front top of the house. Sew a button on each side, using the tie method, where you have pinned. This leaves the ends hanging free and now all you need is a bamboo stick, dowel rod or even a stick to tie up your little house and hang it on the wall.

YOU WILL NEED

- 25 cm of black background fabric
- 25 cm x 30 cm of pellon
- 31 cm x 36 cm of red check backing fabric
- scraps of yellow, red, blue, purple, black and orange fabrics
- embroidery thread: red, green, black
- pinking shears
- size 7 needle
- pins
- ordinary sewing cotton
- cardboard
- tracing paper
- scissors
- two buttons
- iron
- small amount of Vliesofix iron-on adhesive
- pencil
- ruler
- length of dowel or stick

Fig. 1

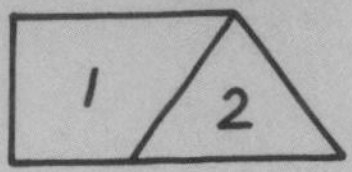

Fig. 2

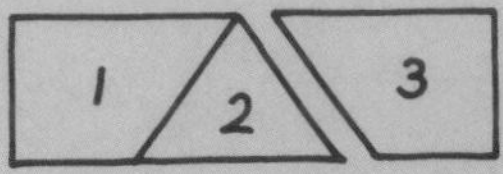

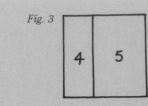

Fig. 3

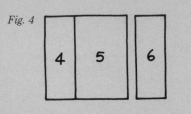

Fig. 4

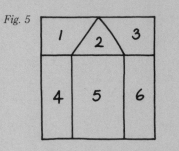

Fig. 5

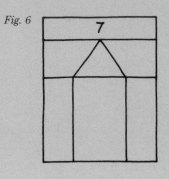

Fig. 6

A tisket, a tasket . . .

YOU WILL NEED
- ■ **6 m of 6 mm thick sisal rope (available from hardware stores)**
- ■ **safety pin, medium-sized**
- ■ **scissors**
- ■ **50 cm of black homespun**
- ■ **50 cm of white homespun**
- ■ **ruler**
- ■ **masking tape**
- ■ **pencil**

These baskets make wonderful gifts and the more you make, the easier they become. At Christmas, I like to fill them with nuts and chocolates. Ben and Jake use theirs to keep their pocket money safe, and Ellie uses hers for her ribbons and bows. If you want to make a larger basket just buy more rope and keep on wrapping!

INSTRUCTIONS

1 Taper one end of the rope with the scissors so that the three coils that make up the rope are separated and at three different lengths (see the close-up picture below).

2 Tape the tapered end with masking tape from about 10 cm down, wrapping it around and around the rope, making sure the end is well covered. Set it aside.

3 Measure along the shortest side of both the black and white homespun fabrics, making a mark every 3 cm. Cut a small nick at each mark with the scissors, then, at every nick, rip the fabric all the way down the length of the fabric. Pull off any fraying bits and make two piles of fabric beside you, one black and one white.

4 Fasten the safety pin at the very end of one of the white fabric strips. Pick up the rope and wrap the other end of the fabric around the masking tape starting about 10 cm from the end of the rope and working back; wrap the fabric over the end point, then start working back up the rope (see the picture on page 48). Each wrap should just cover the last so that no rope is showing. After five wraps along the rope, fold the end piece over

into a tight coil shape and wrap the fabric over two adjoining pieces of rope to hold them together, using the safety pin like a needle.

5 When you run out of white fabric, start the black fabric by overlapping one wrap of the last piece of fabric; do not start a new colour at a joining wrap.

6 Now you can start working your basket. Wrap the fabric three times around the rope, always working away from you, pulling tight each time, then pushing the safety pin through the last row of rope just worked. Wrap it around, pushing the safety pin up over the middle of the joining stitch and back to the start again (see the picture on page 48). This joining stitch holds your work together.

7 Make five complete rounds of the basket – not counting the centre coil. Turn the circular base sideways and continue working in the same fashion, only working from the side and laying your first round

Tapering the rope

of rope directly on top of the last round on the bottom to form an edge. Do a joining stitch every three wraps of fabric and you will start to see a pattern forming. Work six or seven rows up the side, pulling the basket into a round shape as you go.

TO FINISH

When the side is completed, you must taper the end of the rope as you did at the beginning. Finish by wrapping the fabric over the end a couple of times and going into the row below to tie it down. Tuck the fabric inside the basket, making a knot over one of the joining stitches. If this part is not securely tied, the basket will come undone.

Using a joining stitch to make the pattern

FOR THE LID

You can have an open basket, finishing it off by tying a bow over the last stitch worked, or you might like to add a lid.

The lid is worked in exactly the same way as the base of the basket with the same number of rounds. When the lid is the right size, finish it off in the same way as the basket, tapering the end with masking tape as before. To attach the lid you can either tie a bow across the last stitch, joining it to the basket at the same time, or you can just go over the basket and lid together, finishing off on the inside of the basket.

Beginning to wrap the rope at one end

Merry Christmas

INSTRUCTIONS

See the pattern on the Pull Out Pattern Sheet.

For the angel

1. Trace the angel and the two stars and cut out the tracings, then copy them onto the cardboard. Cut the shapes out of the cardboard. These will be your patterns.
2. Place the pattern for the angel onto the right side of one Christmas fabric. Draw around it, then cut the shape with the pinking shears, cutting I cm away from the pencil line. The pencil line is where you will sew. Mark the opening on the fabric. Cut two.
3. The two sets of stars are cut in the same manner as for the angel, using the other Christmas fabric. Cut four stars.
4. Pin the angel pieces to hold them together while you are sewing them. Using two strands of red embroidery thread and a small running stitch, start sewing at one end of the opening mark. Work your way around the pencil line and finish with a back stitch at the other side of the opening mark. If you have some thread in your needle, leave this hanging, but remove your needle first. You can use this thread to close the opening after you have stuffed the angel.
5. Push scraps of wadding, a little at a time, into the ends of the arms and head first. Stuff quite firmly so the angel is stiff and holds itself upright. Stitch up the opening using a strong back stitch.

For the stars

1. Place one of the cut-out stars onto the pellon and cut carefully around the star with the pinking shears, then line up the other cut-out star on the back with both stars facing right side out sort of like a sandwich. Pin the layers to hold them together while you are sewing them.
2. Stitch around the stars with two strands navy thread, sewing along the pencil line. Finish with a back stitch. If any of the pell is hanging out, just trim it away when you have finished. Now, press the stars firmly with a hot iron; this will make them lie fla and will stiffen them.

TO FINISH

1. Tie a button in the centre of each star, using the red thread. Tie another two buttons to the front of the angel.
2. Find the centre of the rickrack braid and place it in the middle of the angel's neck the back. Wrap it around the angel, crossing over under the buttons and und the arms. Do both sides at the same tim then flip the angel over and tie a firm kn at the centre back. Trim off any excess braid.
3. Tie the Christmas ribbon around from t base of the angel's head at the back. It's easier if you pin the ribbon at this point then tie it in a knot at the top of the he on the front. If you stitch a small back st at both these points, the headband will come off. Trim the ribbon to be about cm long and cut a V shape in the end c the ribbons.

ASSEMBLING

Place the two sets of stars at the end of th angel's arms and attach them with a small b stitch, hiding the stitches at the back. Cut th green ribbon in half and stitch one half to e star. Your swag is now ready for hanging ac the front door and will greet your friends a Christmas with a friendly nod!

My name is . . .

YOU WILL NEED

- **two 22 cm x 35 cm pieces natural homespun, (or longer if you have more than five letters in your name – allow 6 cm for each letter)**
- **20 cm x 33 cm of Vliesofix iron-on adhesive**
- **yellow and blue cotton fabric the same length as the homespun**
- **two 8 cm x 35 cm pieces of cream homespun**
- **two 8 cm x 22 cm pieces of cream homespun**
- **two 8 cm x 35 cm pieces of pellon**
- **8 cm x 22 cm each of red and green cotton fabric**
- **two 8 cm x 22 cm pieces of pellon**
- **scraps of other cotton fabrics for the letters**
- **10 cm of Vliesofix iron-on adhesive**
- **thirty-eight odd buttons**
- **embroidery thread: cream, pink**
- **iron**
- **ruler**
- **scissors**
- **pins**
- **cardboard**
- **tracing paper**
- **pencil**

INSTRUCTIONS

See the pattern on page 54.

1. Using the sample letter given as a guide on page 54, draw the letters for your name onto the cardboard. Use a ruler to ensure the lines are perfectly straight. Cut the letters out and place them on the right side of your chosen fabrics for the letters. Draw around them with the pencil.

2. Iron a small piece of Vliesofix from the 10 cm wide piece (sticky side down) onto the back of .each letter, holding the iron down for ten seconds. Carefully cut out the letters along the pencil lines. Peel away the backing on the Vliesofix, then place the letters (Vliesofix side down) in the middle of one of the large homespun pieces. Press with a hot iron for ten seconds as before.

3. Sew around each letter in a running stitch, using two strands of cream embroidery thread. Start and end your sewing on the back of each letter.

4. Iron the large Vliesofix piece (sticky side down) onto the back of the homespun that has your name sewn onto it. This makes the fabric firm, so it will need to be pressed very well. Peel off the backing from the Vliesofix and place the other large homespun piece onto the Vliesofix and iron again. You should now have the homespun with your name sewn on it, the Vliesofix in the middle and the other piece of homespun on the back, all ironed together.

5. Trace the zigzag shape from the pattern. The length of the zigzags depends on the length of your name. Allow one zigzag for each letter. For example, Timothy would have seven zigzags. Cut out the tracing, then copy it onto the cardboard as many times as you need. Cut out the cardboard for your pattern.

6. Pin the blue fabric, a piece of pellon and the same size piece of homespun together. Using the pattern, mark, then cut out the zigzag shape, cutting all three layers at the same time. Sew around the zigzag shape in a running stitch, using two strands of the pink thread. You don't have to sew along the straight edge yet, but keep it pinned.

7. Repeat these steps with the yellow side and then with the other two shorter sides. Press the four sides with a hot iron when you have finished sewing them and trim any excess fabric that looks untidy.

ASSEMBLING

1. Pin the two longer zigzags 1 cm in from the top and bottom edge of the homespun piece with your name. Sew it in place in a small running stitch, making sure each stitch goes through all three layers.

2. Do the same with the two shorter pieces, attaching them to the sides. Keep your work flat and don't pull the stitches too tightly or the name will pucker. When all four sides are stitched, sew the buttons along the top and bottom edges. You could sew buttons on all four sides if you wish. Ellie's sign took thirty-eight buttons altogether, so if your name is longer you will need more.

Hang your name on your door or above your bed.

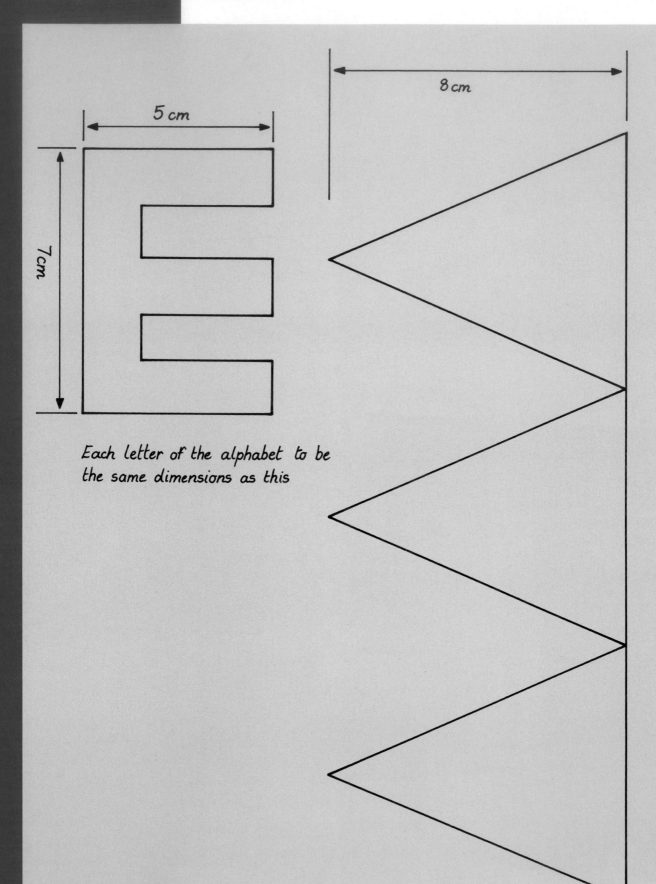

5 cm

8 cm

7cm

Each letter of the alphabet to be the same dimensions as this

Sleeping over dilly bag

INSTRUCTIONS

See the pattern on the Pull Out Pattern Sheet.

1 Lay the black homespun out in one long piece. Fold it in half, crosswise, then iron it exactly along the fold line (Fig. 1). This is the bottom of your bag. Do the same with the lining fabric.

2 Iron the Vliesofix (sticky side down) on the back of the rust/brown fabric, pressing down for ten seconds. Make sure you use a piece of Vliesofix that is big enough for the kangaroo.

3 Trace the kangaroo pattern from the pattern sheet. Cut out the tracing, then copy it onto the cardboard. This will be your pattern. Place the pattern on the right side of the kangaroo material, draw around it and cut it out exactly along the line. Peel the backing off the Vliesofix and iron it onto the front of the black bag about 5 cm up from the bottom fold.

4 Open out the black fabric and stitch around the kangaroo in a neat overstitch, using two strands of red embroidery thread. You could blanket stitch this part if you wish. When you have gone all the way around, finish with a back stitch on the back. Sew on the bead eye.

5 Cut a circle 8 cm in diameter with the pinking shears from the yellow fabric that. Position it above the kangaroo (refer to the picture). Using a running stitch and two strands of black embroidery thread, stitch all the way around the circle. Finish on the back with a back stitch.

6 Ben wrote his name in the circle, then stitched it in running stitch. You can do the same if you like.

7 Measure 33 cm up from the bottom of the bag on the front. Pin one of the yellow strips in position, making sure you place it in the centre. In small running stitches, sew across the top and the bottom of the strip, leaving the ends open for the cord to pass through. Do the same on the back of the bag.

TO FINISH

1 Turn the black bag inside out and fold it double so the right sides are together. Pin, then sew 1 cm in from each side down the length of the bag in a small running stitch, using two strands of black embroidery thread. These two seams can be sewn on the machine if you prefer.

2 Turn the lining bag so the right sides face each other. Pin, then sew both sides as for the black bag. Leave the lining bag as it is but turn the black bag right way out, pushing out the corners with your finger. Now carefully push the lining inside the black bag, matching the side seams together as you go so the bag doesn't twist. Keep pushing until the lining bag is right inside the black bag and both bottoms are together. The lining will be a little longer. Turn the extra length of the lining bag out and over so it makes a little edge at the top of the bag. Turn under a small hem on the lining and pin it so that it stands up about 2 cm above the bag. Using two strands of black embroidery thread, sew running stitches along the hem, sewing through all the layers and starting and finishing on the inside.

YOU WILL NEED

- 35 cm x 84 cm of black homespun
- 34 cm x 92 cm of cotton print fabric for the bag lining
- two 1 m lengths of yellow cord
- two 1 m lengths of red cord
- scrap of yellow fabric
- 25 cm of rust/brown fabric for the kangaroo
- two 5 cm x 30 cm strips of yellow fabric
- safety pin
- bead for the eye
- embroidery thread: red, black
- scissors
- pinking shears
- pins
- pencil
- tracing paper
- 25 cm of Vliesofix iron-on adhesive
- iron
- cardboard

3 Attach a safety pin at the end of one of the yellow cords, then thread it through the yellow strips all the way around and back to the start. Do exactly the same thing with a red cord. Now, with the other yellow and red cords, start at the opposite opening on the bag and thread them all the way around and back to the start (Fig. 2). Tie a big knot about halfway up the hanging cords on each side. Fray the ends by untwisting the cord, if you want a tassel look.

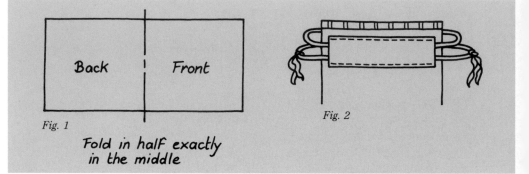

Back   Front

Fig. 1

Fold in half exactly in the middle

Fig. 2

Spooky the lolly bag

YOU WILL NEED

- 18 cm x 60 cm of black homespun
- 5 cm x 18 cm of print fabric (cut with pinking shears)
- 3 cm x 18 cm of a second print fabric (cut with pinking shears)
- 10 cm x 15 cm of white homespun
- 10 cm x 15 cm of Vliesofix iron-on adhesive
- embroidery thread: black, orange
- black permanent fabric marker pen
- beads
- iron
- pinking shears
- scissors
- size 7 needle
- tapestry needle (optional)
- cardboard
- pencil
- ruler
- pins
- tracing paper

INSTRUCTIONS

See the pattern on page 60.

1 Iron the Vliesofix, sticky side down, onto the back of the white homespun, pressing down for ten seconds.

2 Trace the ghost and cut out the tracing. Copy the shape onto the cardboard and cut it out. Place the cardboard pattern onto the Vliesofix side of the homespun and draw around it. Carefully cut exactly along the line, then leave it aside for now.

3 Press the black homespun in half, crosswise. The crease will be the bottom of your bag. Open out the bag again and pin the two print fabric strips into position on the front. To do this, measure down 8 cm from the top edge and draw a line across. Pin the top of the first strip along this line. Then measure down 23 cm from the top of the bag and draw a line across. Pin the top of the second strip along this line (Fig. 1).

4 With two strands of the black embroidery thread and using a running stitch, sew across the top and bottom of the two strips. If you have trouble keeping a straight line then rule one in pencil first and follow it. Finish with a double back stitch at the end of each row before going on to the next. Iron the two strips nice and flat.

For the ghost

Remove the backing from the Vliesofix, and place it, sticky side down, between the two strips. You can position your ghost however you wish, or you can follow the picture. With two strands of black thread and using a small running stitch, sew all the way around the ghost, near the edge, beginning and ending on the back. With the marker pen, draw on a 'spooky' face.

For the bag

1 Fold the black homespun in half again with the right sides together. Pin the sides together, then draw a line 1 cm in from the edge all the way down on both sides. This will be your sewing line. Using two strands of black embroidery thread and a running stitch, sew all the way down one side, starting and finishing with a strong back stitch. Do the same for the other side. Remember if your stitches are too loose or too big all the lollies will fall out! Turn your bag the right way out and iron it flat after gently poking out the corners.

2 Measure down 4 cm from the top and make a pencil mark all the way around the bag. Cut six strands of the orange

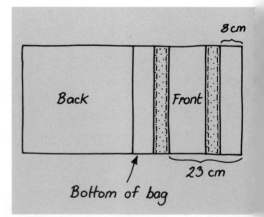

embroidery thread, each 1 m long. If you have trouble threading this thickness, use a tapestry needle. Using a running stitch, slowly sew along the pencil line, starting at the centre front and leaving approximately 40 cm of the thread hanging (you don't need a knot). Keep one hand inside the bag as you work and, when you get back to where you started, pull both sides of the thread to the same length.

3 Thread some beads onto the orange thread on each side, then tie the ends together with a big knot. Cut around the top of the bag with pinking shears or turn under a small hem on the inside of the bag and running stitch around it.

Fill your lolly bag with lots of treats and beware of the spooks lurking inside!

'Moo, moo,' said the cow

INSTRUCTIONS

See the pattern on the Pull Out Pattern Sheet.

For the background

1 Fill the saucepan with boiling water and add the six tea bags. Place one of the large cream homespun pieces into the saucepan, being careful not to burn yourself. Stir the fabric occasionally, allowing it to soak for about twenty minutes. If you want the background colour to be uneven, just screw the fabric up into a ball and hold it together with a rubber band, before putting it in the saucepan. When the water has cooled, take out the fabric and wash it under a cold tap. Wring it out and allow it to dry, then iron it nice and flat.

2 Place the tea-dyed homespun on top of the pellon, face upwards, then place them on top of the other homespun piece. These three layers can be tacked in a large running stitch around the edge, using ordinary cotton.

For the cow

1 Trace the cow's body, head, inner ear and hoof from the pattern sheet. Cut out the tracings, copy them onto the cardboard, then cut out the pattern pieces from the cardboard.

2 Place the pattern pieces for the body and the head on the wrong side of the fabric for the cow. Draw around them with the pencil then cut them out along the pencil line with the pinking shears. Position these pieces in the centre of the tea-dyed homespun and pin them in place with the head on the top right and slightly bent to one side. Cut out the hooves and inner ears from the dark red fabric with pinking shears and pin these on as well.

3 With two strands of black embroidery thread and using a running stitch, sew around the cow, starting at the centre back and removing the pins as you go along. When you reach a hoof just continue sewing as though it were the one piece of material. You can add an extra stitch if you want, then continue around to the udder, going right around this to the next hoof and then up to the head. Keep sewing around the head, beginning at the nose and stitching on the inner red ear as you work. Try to keep your stitches small and not too close to the edge. Sew through all three layers.

4 Make a pattern for the bird as for the cow. Cut out the bird and pin it on top of the cow's back, leaving enough room to draw on the legs. Stitch around the bird in running stitch, using two strands of black thread. Stitch over the drawing of the bird's legs at the same time.

TO FINISH

1 Measure in 3 cm from the edge of the homespun and draw a line all the way around. Using two strands of green embroidery thread, stitch along the four sides on the pencil line in running stitch. Always start and end at the back of your work. Keep your work flat, making sure there are no puckers. You can pin along the pencil line if it helps you to sew straight.

2 Cut out eight 6 cm squares from different brown check fabrics. Pin them to the top and bottom of the hanging, between the

YOU WILL NEED

- two 45 cm x 62 cm pieces of cream homespun
- 45 cm x 62 cm of pellon
- 25 cm of fabric for the cow
- scraps of dark brown check fabric
- small scraps of dark red and brown fabric
- two 5 cm x 30 cm strips of cream homespun
- 8-ply black wool
- raffia
- eight different buttons
- two blue beads for the eyes
- six tea bags
- large saucepan
- embroidery thread: black, green
- size 7 needle
- pencil
- ruler
- scissors
- pinking shears
- iron
- cardboard
- pins
- ordinary sewing cotton
- tracing paper
- stick for hanging

61

lines of green sewing. You can do more squares or place them differently, if you wish. Tie a button in the centre of some of the squares and stitch around the others.

3   Make a plait with twelve 25 cm strands of the wool. Start by knotting them together at one end then holding the knotted end between your legs while you plait for about 20 cm, then tie another knot. Fray the wool that is left hanging at the end of the tail. Trim around the knot, then using black thread sew the tail to the top of the cow's back, going over the knot a few times. Then stitch down the knot at the other end of the tail. The tail between the knots need not be sewn down.

4   Tie on two brown buttons for the cow's nostrils and the two beads for the eyes.

5   Bundle up a little pile of raffia and stitch it to the cow's mouth (under the button nostrils) by sewing over the middle of the bundle several times with black thread.

6   Fold the two homespun strips in half and pin them to the back at the top back – one at each side – for hanging. Attach them by sewing a back stitch five times in the pin spot, using ordinary cotton. Remove the pin when you are finished. Leave the loose ends free to allow you to tie a knot when you hang your cow on a piece of stick.

'Moo, Moo,' said the cow.

I luv Kitty

YOU WILL NEED

- **33 cm x 45 cm of cream cotton fabric for the background**
- **33 cm x 45 cm of wadding**
- **40 cm x 52 cm of red fabric for the backing**
- **25 cm of fabric for the cat**
- **scraps of purple, red and black fabric**
- **red felt for the nose**
- **craft glue**
- **twenty black buttons**
- **embroidery thread: black, white**
- **black permanent fabric marker pen**
- **scissors**
- **pins**
- **size 7 needle**
- **cardboard**
- **pencil**
- **iron**
- **tracing paper**

INSTRUCTIONS

See the pattern on the Pull Out Pattern Sheet.

1   Trace the pattern from the pattern sheet. Cut out the tracings and copy them onto the cardboard.
2   Place the pattern for the cat's head and body on the right side of the cat fabric. Draw around them, then cut them out exactly along the pencil line.
3   Pin the cat's body in the centre of the background fabric. Position the head on top, overlapping the body by about 1 cm, and pin it in place. Using two strands of white embroidery thread and a running stitch, sew around the cat, working close to the edge and starting at the base of the head. For the inner outline of the cat's left foreleg, sew a running stitch 2 cm from the edge of the cat and working up the body. When you have sewn all the way around the body, do a back stitch on the back, then continue with a running stitch around the head. Finish on the back with a strong back stitch.
4   Prepare and cut the whiskers as for the cat's body. Position the whiskers – three on each side – pin them, then sew them in place with a running stitch and two strands of black thread. Cut the nose out of the red felt and glue it between the whiskers with a little craft glue. Using the marker pen, draw on the eyes and colour them in.

For the words

Trace and cut out the letters from the red fabric as before. Position them around Kitty, leaving room around the edge for the border to overlap 2 cm. Pin these into place and, using a running stitch and two strands of black embroidery thread, sew around each letter. Always begin and end on the back of your work. If you have trouble sewing along the letters draw a line first with a pencil and ruler, then sew along the line.

ASSEMBLING

1   Place the wadding in the centre of the red backing fabric, then place the cat piece on top (with the cat facing you). Pin the three layers together to hold them in position. Fold over the red edges onto the top, making a neat 2 cm wide border. Pin the border down, tucking in the corners and ironing as you go; this will help hold it in place while you pin. Try to keep the borders an even width if you can.
2   Mark the positions of the buttons with a pencil so the spaces are even. Using two strands of red embroidery thread, sew on the buttons, sewing on the four corners first, then the middle ones on each side, then the rest of the buttons. This order helps to keep the red fabric lying flat without puckering. The buttons should be sewn on from the back and the thread must go through all the layers: the red backing, then the wadding, then the cat piece, and lastly the red border. Do this about six times and finish off on the back. Each button is sewn on individually.
3   With two strands of black embroidery thread, and using a running stitch, sew around Kitty – going all the way through to the back, if you can. This is a quilting stitch and will help make Kitty stand out from the background. Two small round hooks can be sewn on the back to hang your work or you can put a blob of Blu-Tack in each corner to hold it on the wall, but check with Mum first.

Jake's four patches

YOU WILL NEED

- **50 cm of cream homespun**
- **25 cm each of at least eight different cotton fabrics**
- **60 cm square of fabric for the backing**
- **56 cm square of wadding**
- **10 cm of Vliesofix iron-on adhesive**
- **embroidery thread: black, gold**
- **iron**
- **scissors**
- **pins**
- **sewing needle**
- **ordinary sewing cotton**
- **tracing paper**
- **cardboard**
- **pencil**

INSTRUCTIONS

See the patterns on the Pull Out Pattern Sheet.

Trace all the pattern pieces for the four different blocks. Cut them out and copy them onto the cardboard. Number them as you see them on the pattern. These will be your pattern pieces. Make sure each block measures 20 cm square when you have drawn it.

Block one

1   Cut out a heart and a square pattern piece from the cardboard. Place the square on the back of your four chosen fabrics and draw around it with the pencil. This pencil line is where you will sew.

2   Cut the squares out of the fabric, adding 1 cm all around each piece as you cut.

3   Assemble the block, following the number order set out in figure 1 and stitch in a small running stitch, using ordinary cotton. Begin and end your sewing with a back stitch. You will need to pin two pieces together first, so that you sew exactly along the pencil line. Check that your sewing stays on the line or your block will not be the right size when it is finished. Press with a hot iron.

4   Cut a square of Vliesofix slightly larger than you need for the heart. Place the Vliesofix onto the back of the fabric with the sticky side down. Press the Vliesofix onto the fabric with a hot iron, pressing down for ten seconds. Draw around the heart pattern onto the ironed piece. Cut the heart out exactly along the line you have drawn. Peel the backing paper off the Vliesofix and iron the heart onto the fabric square with the sticky side down, pressing for ten seconds. Do this for all four squares.

5   Using two strands of gold thread, stitch the hearts in place with an overstitch.

Block two

Cut out all the pattern pieces from the fabric in the same way as you did for block one.

1   Sew 1 + 2 together four times (Fig. 2).

2   Join the four little squares to make a larger square (Fig. 3). Be careful to arrange the squares as you see them in the photograph.

3   Join a 3 to each side of the large square (Fig. 4).

4   Join a 5 to either end of the 4 (Fig. 5).

5   Join the 6 to the bottom (Fig. 6).

6   Join the two halves together to complete the block (Fig. 7).

Block three

Cut out all the pattern pieces from the fabric in the same way as you did for block one.

1   Join 3 + 1 (Fig. 8).

2   Join 2 + 3 (Fig. 9).

3   Join 3 + 1 to 2 + 3 (Fig. 10).

4   Sew a 6 to the top of 3 + 1 + 2 + 3 (Fig. 11).

5   Sew 4 + 5 together (Fig. 12).

6   Join 4 + 5 to the bottom of the main joined piece to complete the block (Fig. 13).

7   Attach the door, window and chimney in the same way as you attached the heart on block one.

Block four

Cut out all the pattern pieces from the fabric in the same way as you did for block one.

1   Sew 1 + 2 together four times (Fig. 14).
2   Join a 1 + 2 with a 3 in between, twice (Fig. 15).
3   Sew a 4 to either end of a 5 (Fig. 16).
4   Join the three strips to form the complete block (Fig. 17).

TO FINISH

1   With a pencil, mark six strips of homespun, each 4 cm × 20 cm. Cut these out, adding a 1 cm seam allowance all around each one.
2   Pin two blocks and three homespun strips with the right sides together as shown in figure 18. Do this twice.
3   Sew the blocks and strips together along the pencil line in ordinary cotton with a running stitch. Begin and end with a double back stitch.
4   Measure and draw three pieces of homespun, each 4 cm × 54 cm. Cut these out, adding 1 cm seam allowances as before. Pin the three long strips and the block strips you have already joined with the right sides together as shown in figure 19. Stitch them together in a small running stitch in ordinary cotton exactly along the pencil line, beginning and ending with a double back stitch.
5   When the top is all sewn together, press it with a hot iron and trim away any excess fabric to make your patchwork nice and square.
6   Place the backing fabric, right side down on a table or on the floor. Place the wadding next, then the top (right side up) in the centre of the wadding. Pin all three layers together.
7   Fold the backing fabric over the top of the other two, making a border on the top (Fig. 20). Turn under a small hem at the same time. If you find this step too difficult, perhaps Mum will lend a hand. Pin the border down all the way around. In two strands of black embroidery thread, stitch in a small running stitch along the hem line. This does not have to go through to the back. (I like to work on the floor when doing this part, but be careful not to lose any pins.) When you reach the corners, tuck them under and stitch them down, taking out the pins as you go.
8   To hold the quilt layers together, sew a small cross in the black embroidery thread on the corner of each block. To do this, start with a knot on the back, come up and stitch a small cross, go to the back and then finish off. Repeat for the next corner and so on. Do this as often as you like and this will help your little quilt to stay together forever.

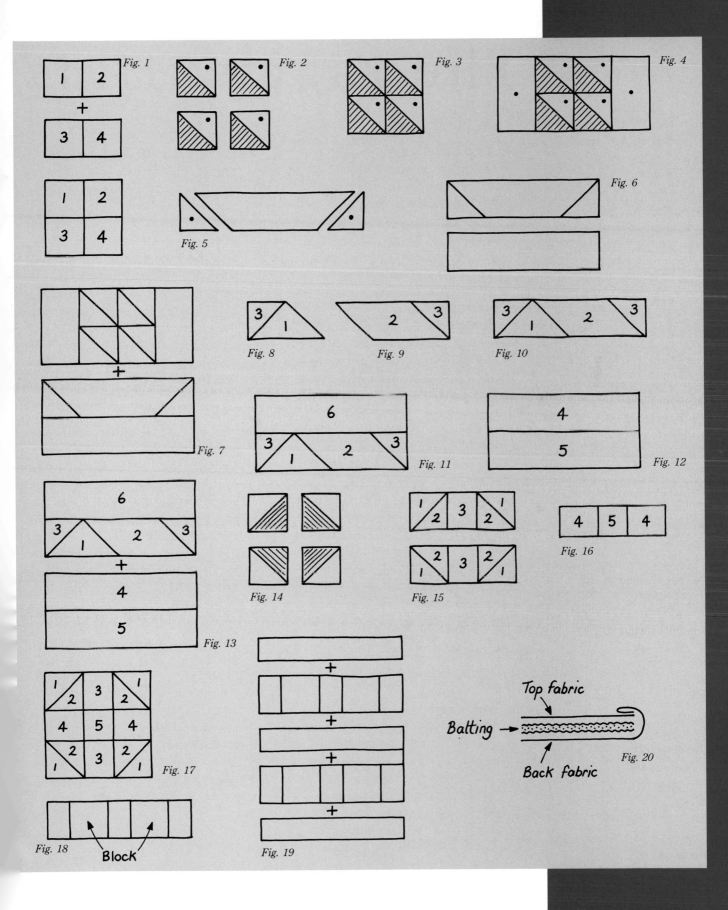

Fig. 1
Fig. 2
Fig. 3
Fig. 4
Fig. 5
Fig. 6
Fig. 7
Fig. 8
Fig. 9
Fig. 10
Fig. 11
Fig. 12
Fig. 13
Fig. 14
Fig. 15
Fig. 16
Fig. 17
Fig. 18 Block
Fig. 19
Fig. 20
Top fabric
Batting
Back fabric

The ragamuffins

YOU WILL NEED

For the black doll
- 25 cm of black homespun
- 25 cm of fabric for the dress
- two buttons for the eyes
- 8-ply black wool for the hair
- embroidery thread: red, black
- ordinary sewing cotton, black

For the white doll
- 25 cm of white homespun
- 25 cm of fabric for the dress
- small piece of fabric for the apron
- two buttons for the eyes
- cream mohair wool for the hair
- embroidery thread: red, white
- ordinary sewing cotton, white
- 1 m of pink ribbon
- 38 cm of cream lace
- tapestry needle

For both
- cardboard
- pencil
- tracing paper
- scissors
- pinking shears
- pins
- size 7 needle
- stuffing

INSTRUCTIONS
See the patterns on pages 73-75.

FOR THE BLACK DOLL

1 Trace the doll pattern from the pattern sheet. Cut out the tracing and copy it onto the cardboard. Cut the pattern piece out of the cardboard.
2 Fold the black homespun over so it is doubled. Place the pattern on the right side of the homespun and draw around the shape. Mark the opening on the leg with the pencil. With the pinking shears, cut out around the doll 1 cm from the pencil line. The pencil line is where you will sew.
3 Pin the two pieces together around the outside edge. Then, with two strands of black embroidery thread and starting with a strong back stitch, sew along the pencil line with small running stitches. Begin at one side of the opening mark and finish at the other side of the mark with a back stitch. Do not cut off the thread, but leave it hanging.
4 Take some stuffing and gently push it into the head and outer arm first – a little at a time – until the doll is firmly stuffed. Now sew up the opening with the hanging thread and do a strong back stitch to finish. Trim the edge if needed.

For the dress

1 Make a cardboard pattern for the dress as for the doll. Fold the dress material over double with the right sides together. Place the pattern on the fabric with the shoulder part on the fold. Cut out the dress, leaving a 1 cm seam allowance. Cut the bottom of the dress with pinking shears.

2 Pin the two sides and the arm seams, then stitch with the ordinary cotton in a small running stitch. End with a back stitch. Turn the dress the right way out.
3 With two strands of embroidery thread and a running stitch, start on the inside neck and stitch around the opening, about 5 mm from the edge. When you get back to the beginning knot, pop the dress over the doll's head and pull the thread up tightly around the doll's neck. Do two back stitches to hold it tight and hide your thread under the dress. The sleeves are sewn in exactly the same way.

For the hair

1 Mark the five positions for the hair on the doll's head and cut five pieces of homespun, each 2 cm x 10 cm. Fold each piece in half and pin the middle of it to one of the marks on the head. Sew on each piece with a back stitch going over the same spot five times.
2 Cut the black wool into five bundles of ten 10 cm lengths of wool each. Place these in the middle of the homespun strips and tie them into a firm knot (Fig. 1). Make sure the knot is tied tightly or the wool will fall out.

TO FINISH
Sew on two buttons for the eyes, using the tie method and the red embroidery thread. For the mouth, push your needle in from the back and sew a cross, then take your thread to the back again and do a back stitch. You might like to draw the mouth on in pencil first, so you know where to sew.

FOR THE WHITE DOLL

Follow steps 1-4 as for the black doll, using the white homespun and white cotton.

For the dress

1 Make the dress in the same way as for the black doll. Pin the cream lace to the bottom of the doll's dress, then stitch it in a running stitch in ordinary cotton. Overlap the lace slightly where the ends meet and finish off the stitching on the inside.

2 Trace the apron pattern and draw it onto cardboard as before. Fold the apron fabric over double and place the pattern on the doubled fabric with the shoulders on the fold line. Cut out the apron with ordinary scissors . Make a mark where the ribbon ties will go on each side. Cut four pieces of ribbon, each 18 cm long. Back stitch one end of each one to the marks on the apron. Pop the apron over the dress and tie the ribbons on each side in a big bow.

For the hair

Cut a long length of the mohair wool and put a knot in one end. You will need to use the tapestry needle for this part. Starting at the base of the head, do a loose overstitch all the way around the head (Fig. 2). The hair should stand out about 3 cm from the head – don't pull your thread tightly, just stitch slowly in and out, leaving 3 cm loose each time you do a stitch. When you reach the end, do a back stitch carefully without pulling the other stitches. The mohair gives a nice 'woolly' look to the hair, and the rough texture of the wool will stop it from slipping. I would not recommend a smooth wool for this type of stitch.

Finish as for the black doll.

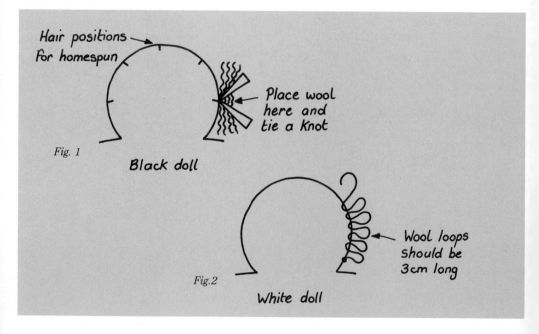

Fig. 1

Black doll

Hair positions for homespun

Place wool here and tie a knot

Wool loops should be 3 cm long

Fig.2

White doll

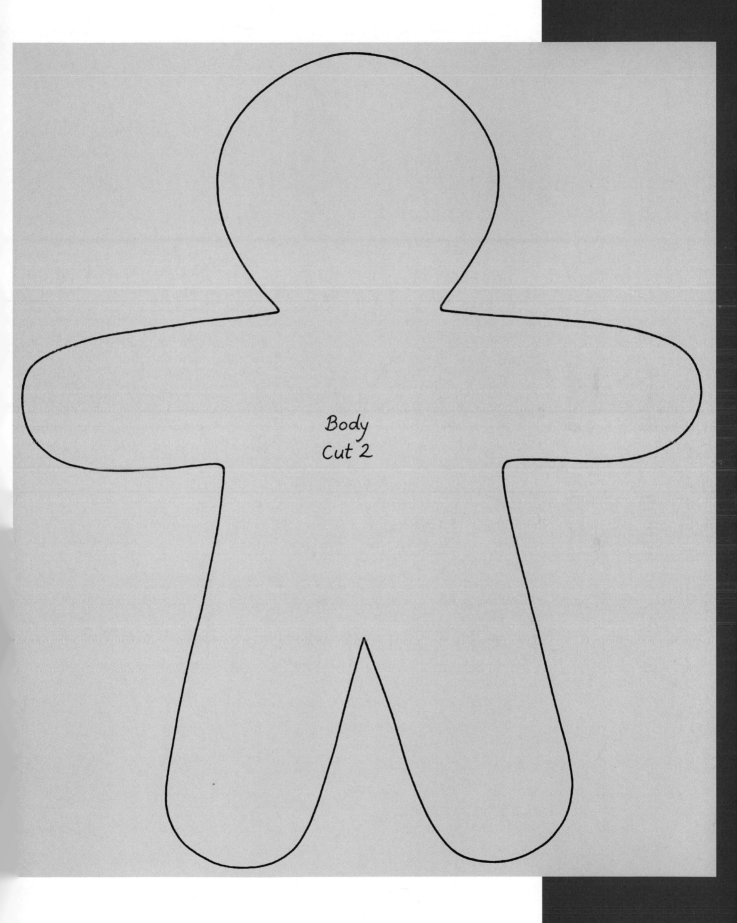

Body
Cut 2

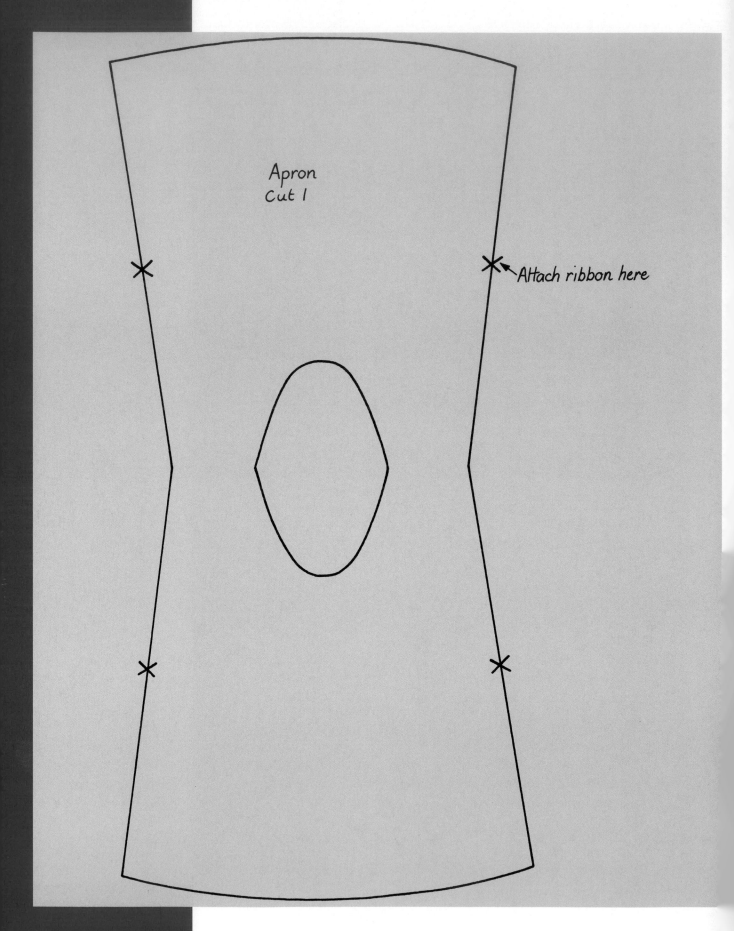

Apron
Cut 1

Attach ribbon here